LET THE WILD RUMPUS START!

GRAPHIC BIOGRAPHIES

ELIZABETH CADY STANTON

WOMEN'S RIGHTS PIONEER

by Connie Colwell Miller

illustrated by Cynthia Martin

Consultant:

Melodie Andrews, PhD

ociate Professor of Early American History and Women's History

Minnesota State University, Mankato

Capstone
press

Mankato, Minnesota

Graphic Library is published by Capstone Press,
151 Good Counsel Drive, P.O. Box 669, Mankato, Minnesota 56002.
www.capstonepress.com

Printed in the United States of America

1 2 3 4 5 6 10 09 08 07 06 05

Library of Congress Cataloging-in-Publication Data
Miller, Connie Colwell, 1976–
Elizabeth Cady Stanton: women's rights pioneer / by Connie Colwell Miller; illustrated by Cynthia Martin.
p. cm. — (Graphic library. Graphic biographies)
Summary: "Describes the life and career of suffragist Elizabeth Cady Stanton"—Provided by publisher.
Includes bibliographical references and index.
ISBN 0-7368-4971-8 (hardcover)
1. Stanton, Elizabeth Cady, 1815–1902—Juvenile literature. 2. Feminists—United States—Biography—Juvenile literature. 3. Suffragists—United States—Biography—Juvenile literature. 4. Women's rights—United States—History—Juvenile literature. 5. Women—Suffrage—United States—History—Juvenile literature. I. Martin, Cynthia. II. Title. III. Series.
HQ1413.S67M55 2006
305.42'092—dc22 2005009211

Art and Editorial Direction
Jason Knudson and Blake A. Hoena

Designers
Jason Knudson and Jennifer Bergstrom

Colorist
Cynthia Martin

Inker
Keith Tucker

Editor
Angie Kaelberer

Editor's note: Direct quotations from primary sources are indicated by a yellow background.

Direct quotations appear on the following pages:
Page 5 from *Eighty Years and More (1815–1897): Reminiscenses of Elizabeth Cady Stanton,* by Elizabeth Cady Stanton. (New York: Source Book Press, 1970.)
Pages 12, 20, and 25 from *In Her Own Right: The Life of Elizabeth Cady Stanton*, by Elisabeth Griffith. (New York: Oxford University Press, 1984.)
Pages 13, 16, 18, 19, and 23 from *The Elizabeth Cady Stanton–Susan B. Anthony Reader: Correspondence, Writings, Speeches*, edited by Ellen Carol DuBois. (Boston: Northeastern University Press, 1981.)

TABLE OF CONTENTS

CHAPTER 1

AN INDEPENDENT GIRL

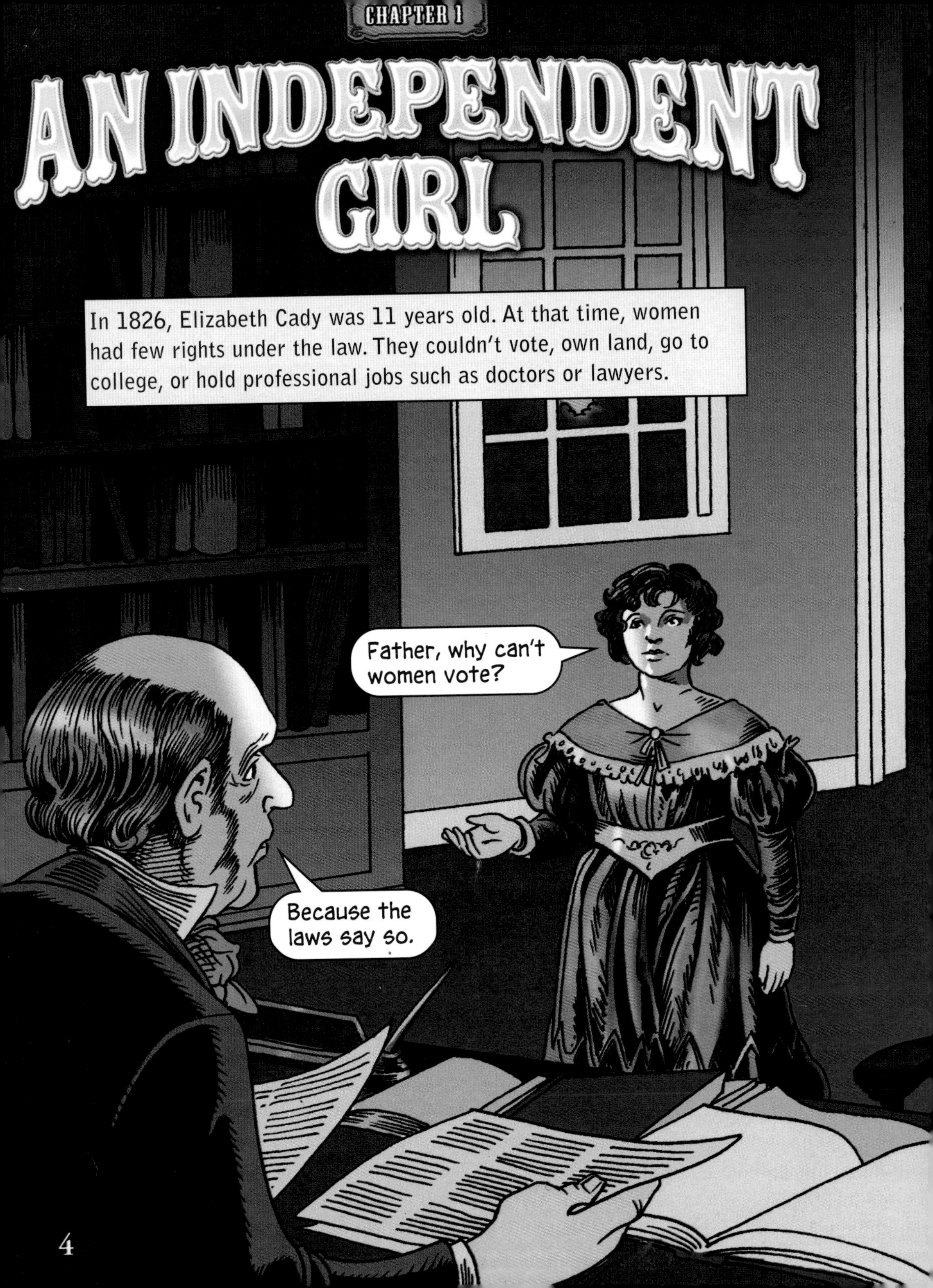
In 1826, Elizabeth Cady was 11 years old. At that time, women had few rights under the law. They couldn't vote, own land, go to college, or hold professional jobs such as doctors or lawyers.
Father, why can't women vote?
Because the laws say so.

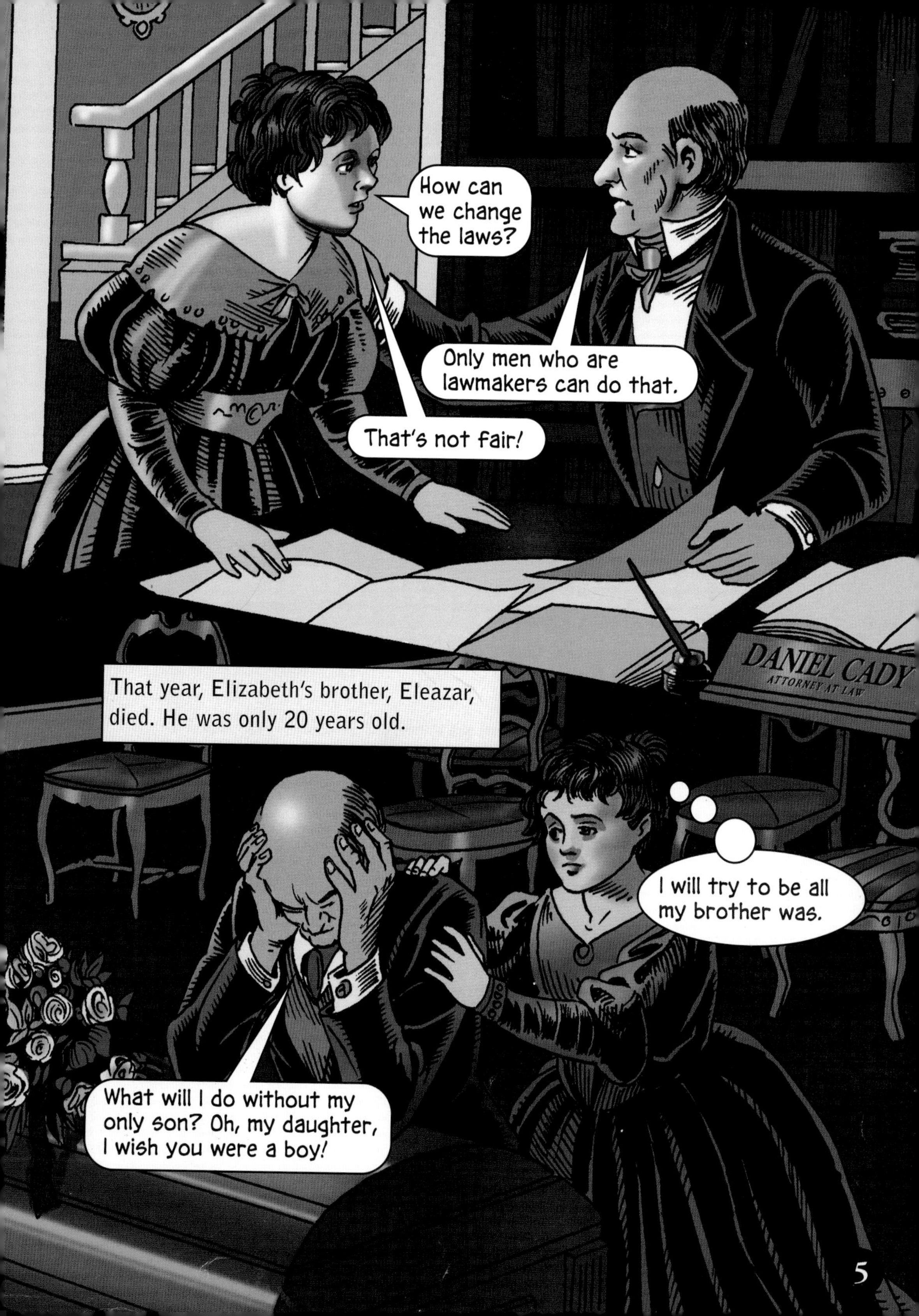
How can we change the laws?
Only men who are lawmakers can do that.
That's not fair!
DANIEL CADY
ATTORNEY AT LAW
That year, Elizabeth's brother, Eleazar, died. He was only 20 years old.
What will I do without my only son? Oh, my daughter, I wish you were a boy!
I will try to be all my brother was.

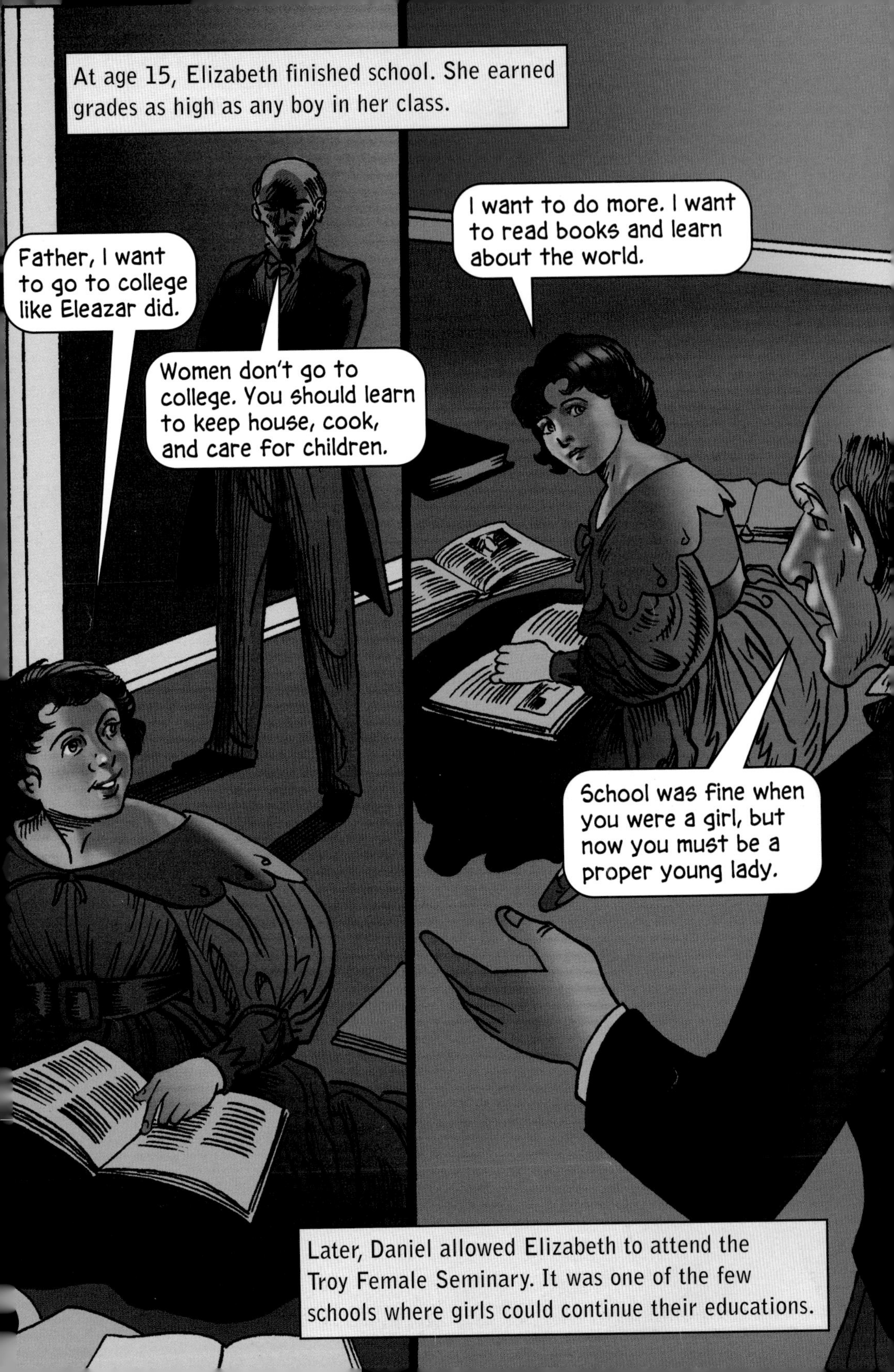
At age 15, Elizabeth finished school. She earned grades as high as any boy in her class.
Father, I want to go to college like Eleazar did.
Women don't go to college. You should learn to keep house, cook, and care for children.
I want to do more. I want to read books and learn about the world.
School was fine when you were a girl, but now you must be a proper young lady.
Later, Daniel allowed Elizabeth to attend the Troy Female Seminary. It was one of the few schools where girls could continue their educations.

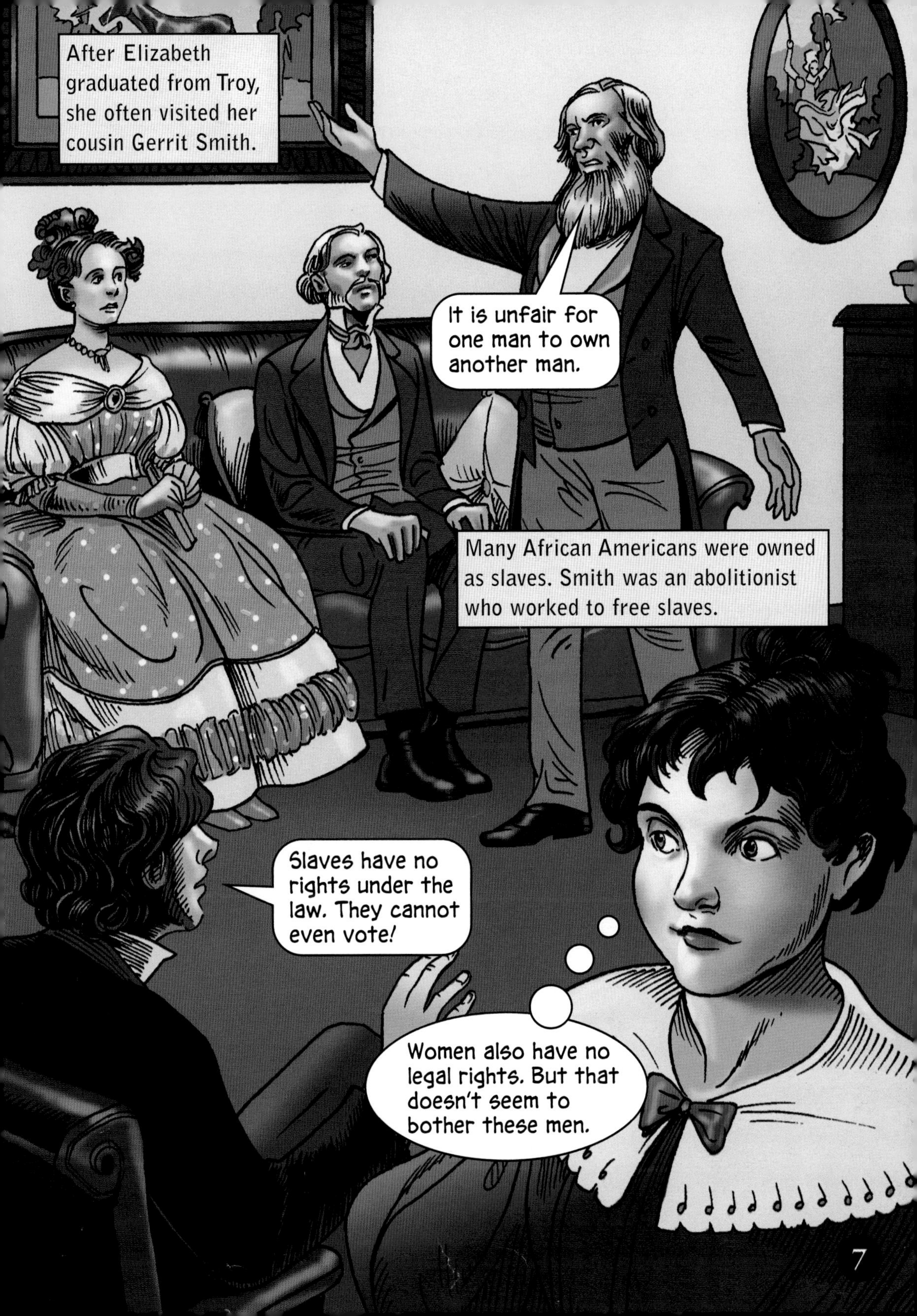
After Elizabeth graduated from Troy, she often visited her cousin Gerrit Smith.
It is unfair for one man to own another man.
Many African Americans were owned as slaves. Smith was an abolitionist who worked to free slaves.
Slaves have no rights under the law. They cannot even vote!
Women also have no legal rights. But that doesn't seem to bother these men.

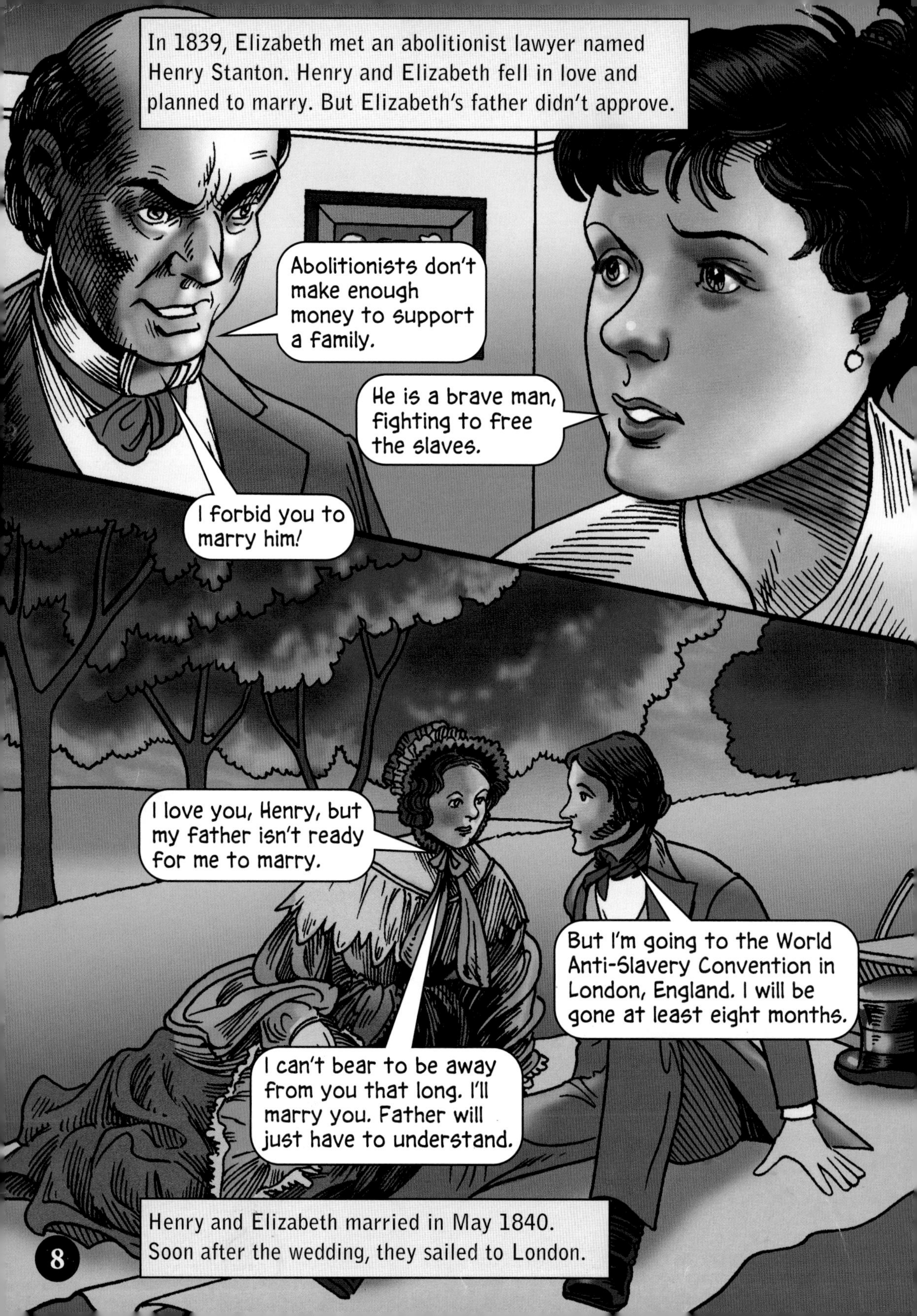
In 1839, Elizabeth met an abolitionist lawyer named Henry Stanton. Henry and Elizabeth fell in love and planned to marry. But Elizabeth's father didn't approve.
Abolitionists don't make enough money to support a family.
He is a brave man, fighting to free the slaves.
I forbid you to marry him!
I love you, Henry, but my father isn't ready for me to marry.
But I'm going to the World Anti-Slavery Convention in London, England. I will be gone at least eight months.
I can't bear to be away from you that long. I'll marry you. Father will just have to understand.
Henry and Elizabeth married in May 1840. Soon after the wedding, they sailed to London.

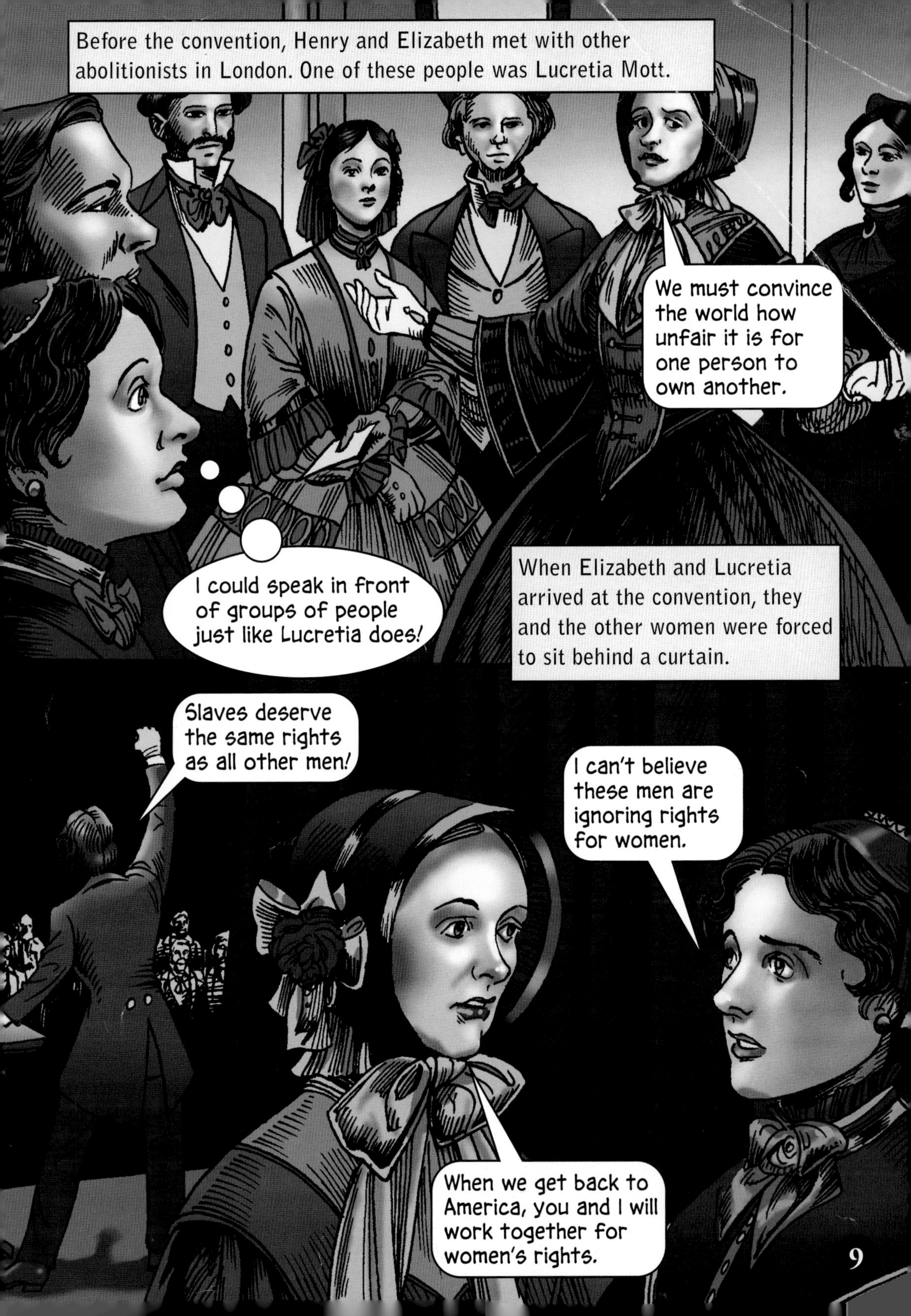

Before the convention, Henry and Elizabeth met with other abolitionists in London. One of these people was Lucretia Mott.
We must convince the world how unfair it is for one person to own another.
I could speak in front of groups of people just like Lucretia does!
When Elizabeth and Lucretia arrived at the convention, they and the other women were forced to sit behind a curtain.
Slaves deserve the same rights as all other men!
I can't believe these men are ignoring rights for women.
When we get back to America, you and I will work together for women's rights.

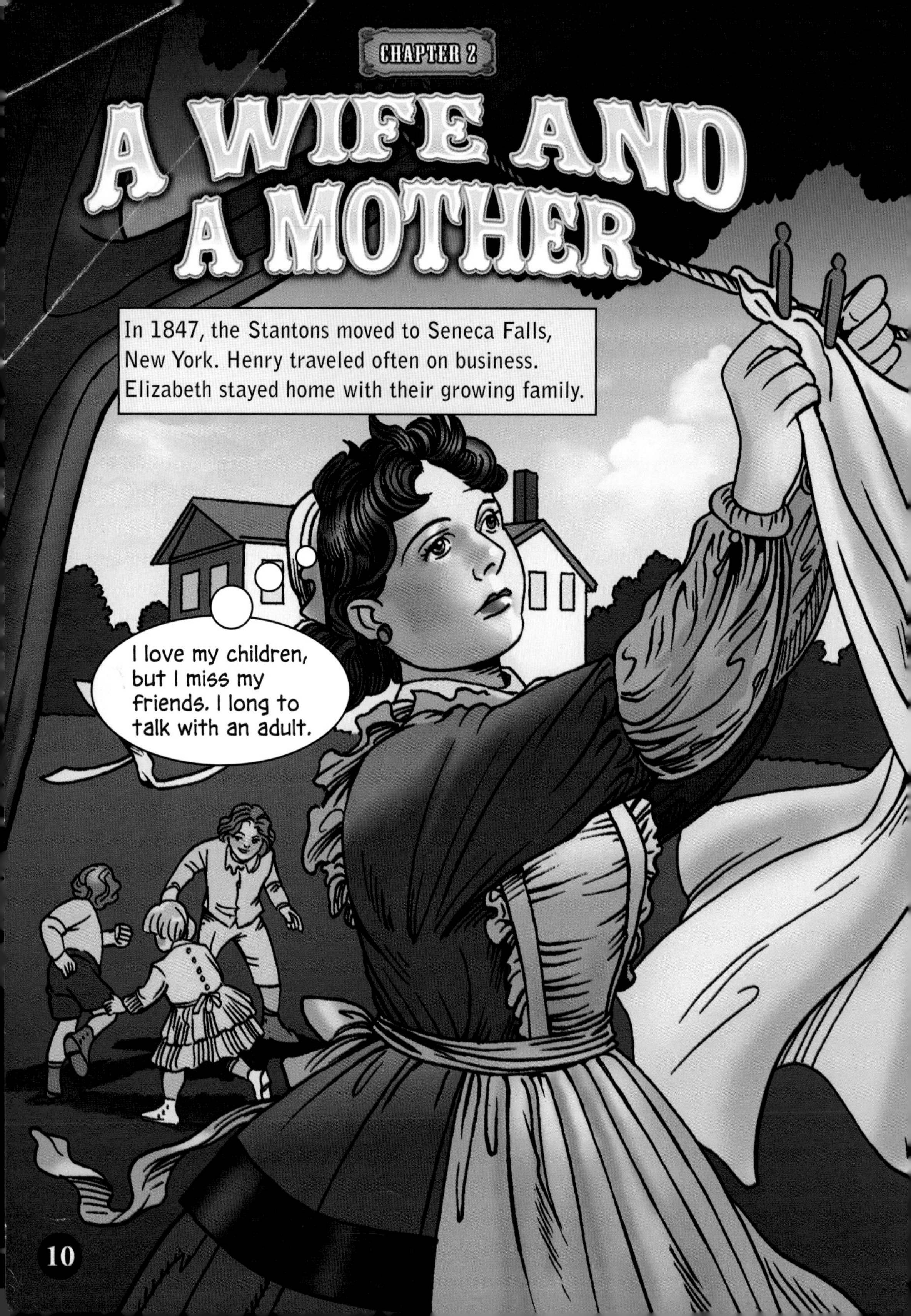
CHAPTER 2
A WIFE AND A MOTHER
In 1847, the Stantons moved to Seneca Falls, New York. Henry traveled often on business. Elizabeth stayed home with their growing family.
I love my children, but I miss my friends. I long to talk with an adult.

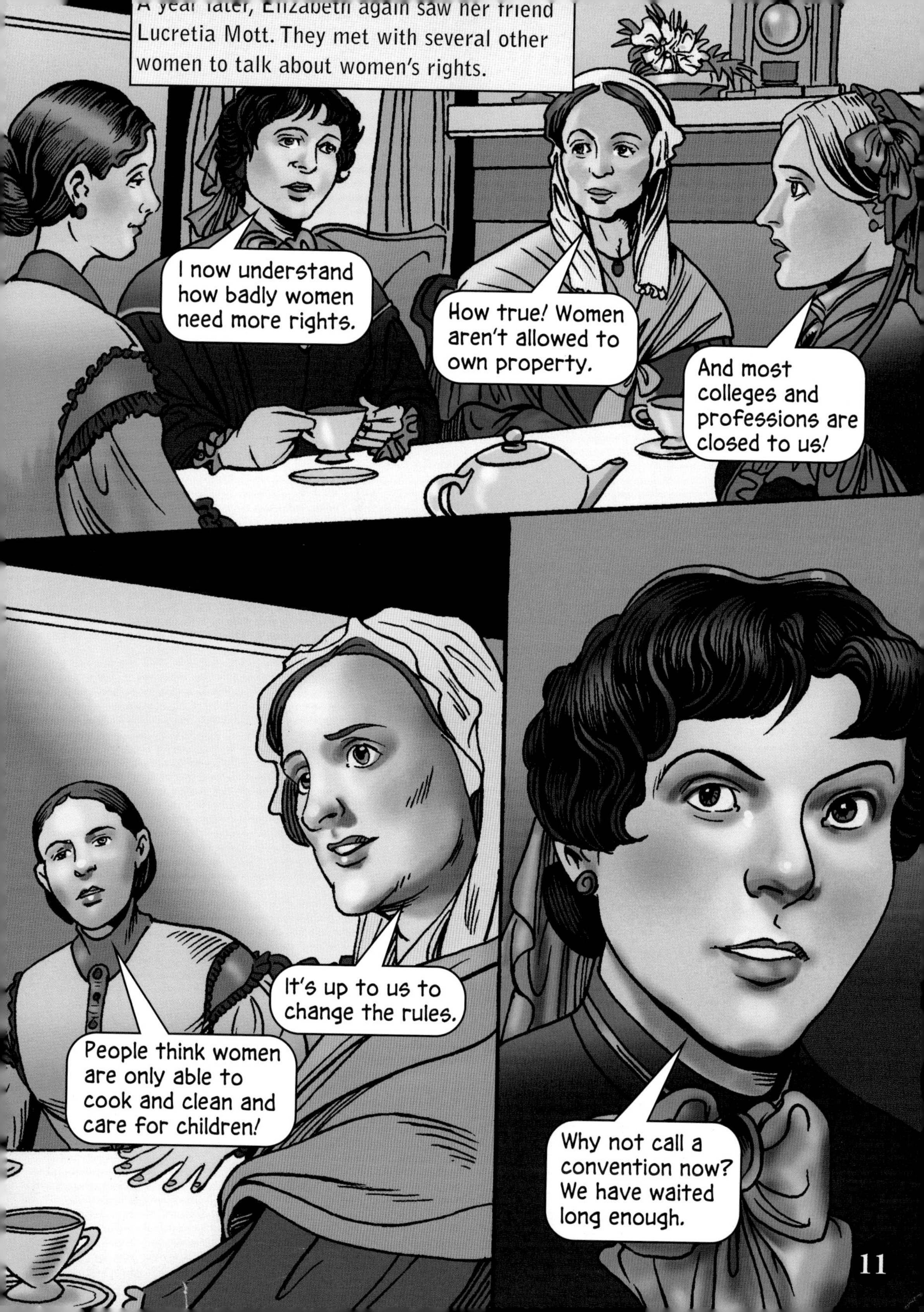
A year later, Elizabeth again saw her friend Lucretia Mott. They met with several other women to talk about women's rights.
I now understand how badly women need more rights.
How true! Women aren't allowed to own property.
And most colleges and professions are closed to us!
It's up to us to change the rules.
People think women are only able to cook and clean and care for children!
Why not call a convention now? We have waited long enough.

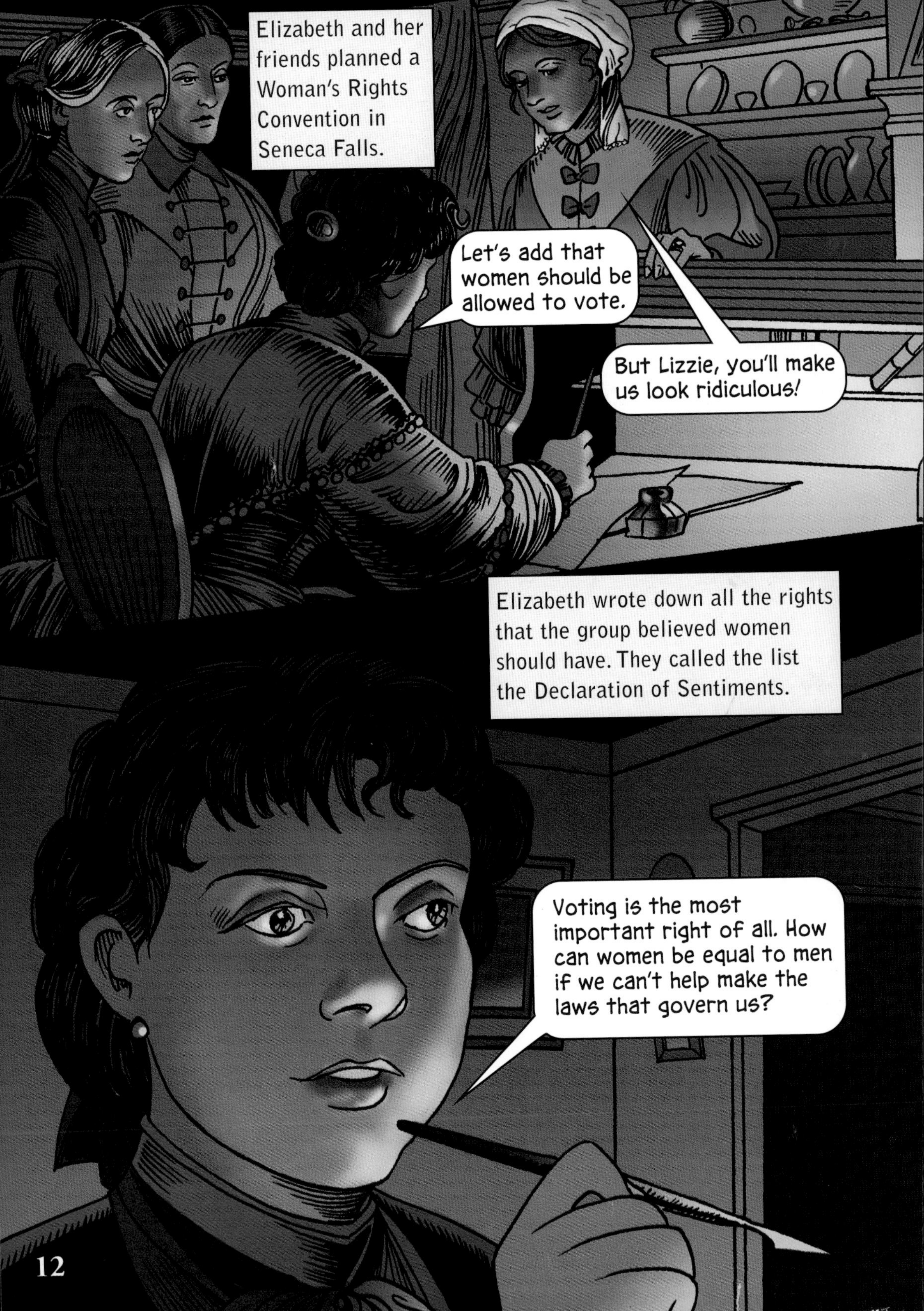
Elizabeth and her friends planned a Woman's Rights Convention in Seneca Falls.
Let's add that women should be allowed to vote.
But Lizzie, you'll make us look ridiculous!
Elizabeth wrote down all the rights that the group believed women should have. They called the list the Declaration of Sentiments.
Voting is the most important right of all. How can women be equal to men if we can't help make the laws that govern us?

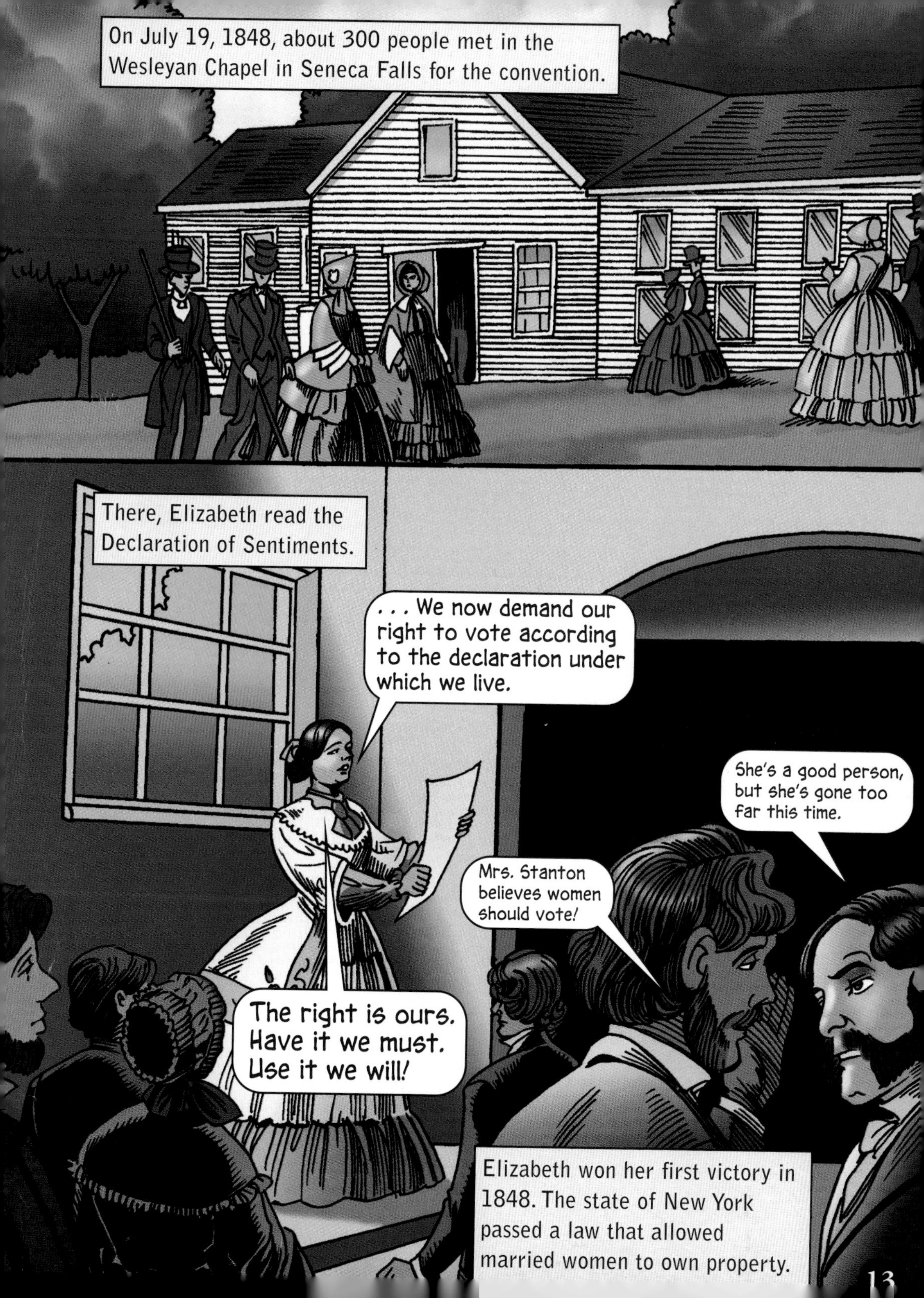

On July 19, 1848, about 300 people met in the Wesleyan Chapel in Seneca Falls for the convention.
There, Elizabeth read the Declaration of Sentiments.
. . . We now demand our right to vote according to the declaration under which we live.
The right is ours. Have it we must. Use it we will!
Mrs. Stanton believes women should vote!
She's a good person, but she's gone too far this time.
Elizabeth won her first victory in 1848. The state of New York passed a law that allowed married women to own property.

Elizabeth hoped to continue writing and delivering speeches for women's rights. But her plans were interrupted when she had two more babies.

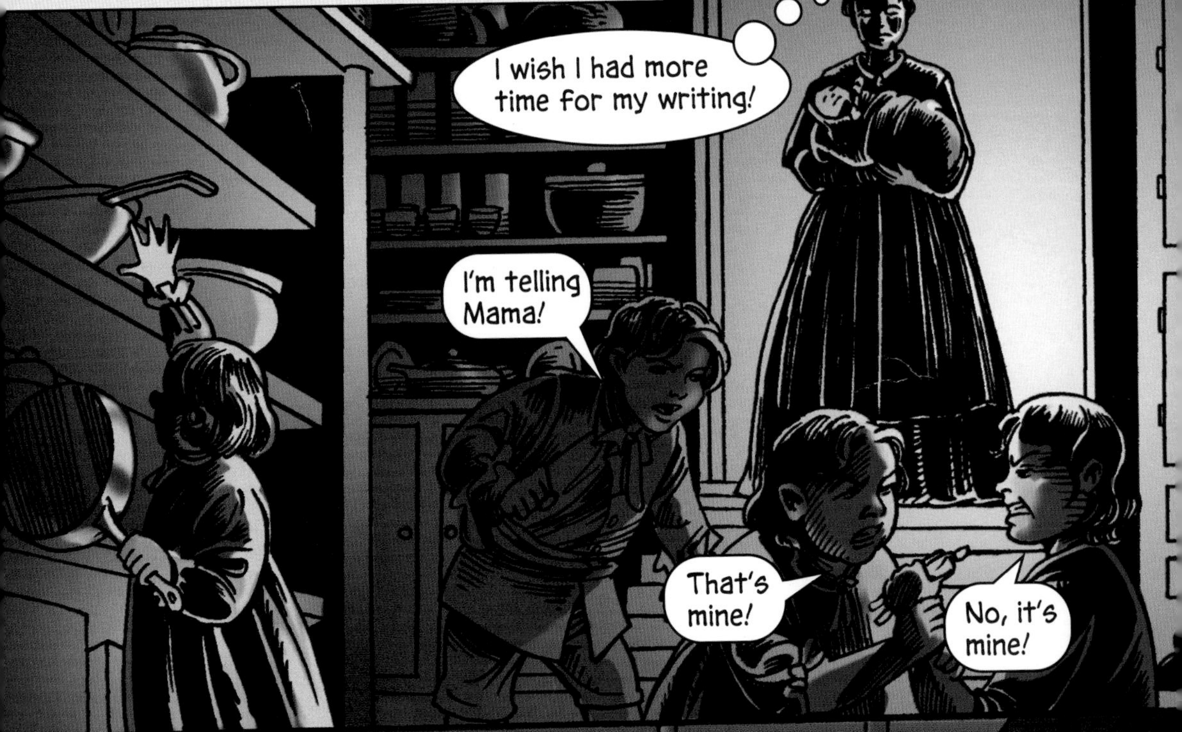
I wish I had more time for my writing!
I'm telling Mama!
That's mine!
No, it's mine!

In 1851, Elizabeth's friend Amelia Bloomer introduced her to Susan B. Anthony. All three women were interested in women's rights.

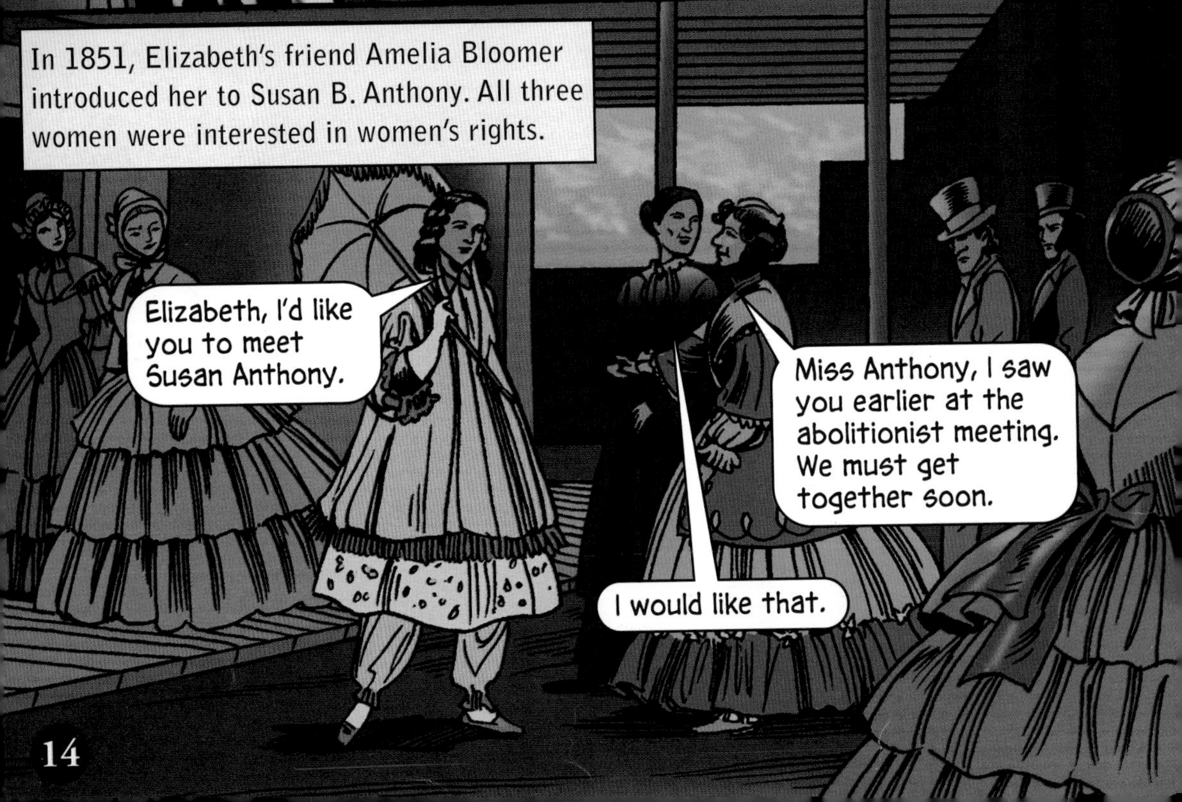
Elizabeth, I'd like you to meet Susan Anthony.
Miss Anthony, I saw you earlier at the abolitionist meeting. We must get together soon.
I would like that.

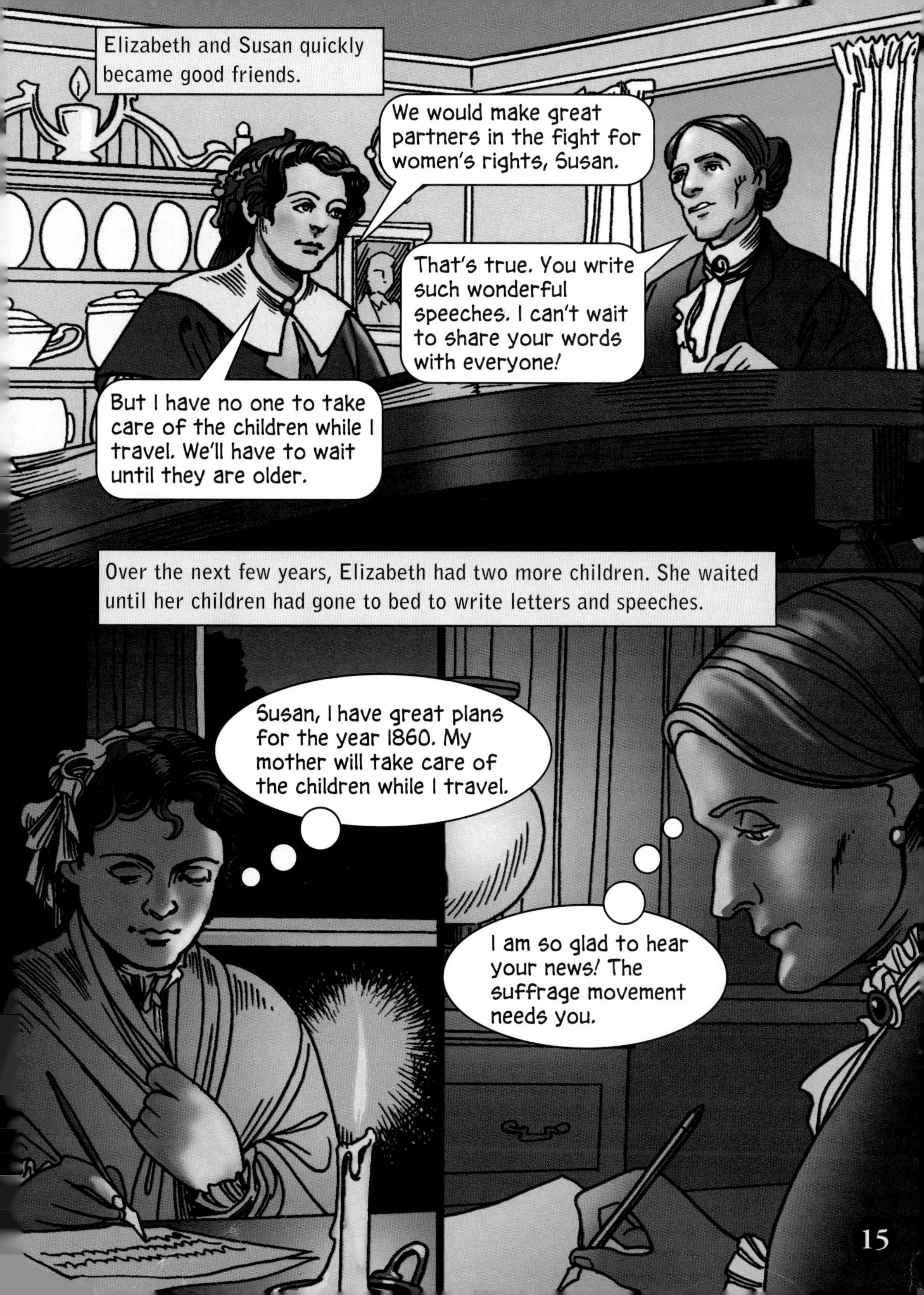
Elizabeth and Susan quickly became good friends.
We would make great partners in the fight for women's rights, Susan.
That's true. You write such wonderful speeches. I can't wait to share your words with everyone!
But I have no one to take care of the children while I travel. We'll have to wait until they are older.
Over the next few years, Elizabeth had two more children. She waited until her children had gone to bed to write letters and speeches.
Susan, I have great plans for the year 1860. My mother will take care of the children while I travel.
I am so glad to hear your news! The suffrage movement needs you.

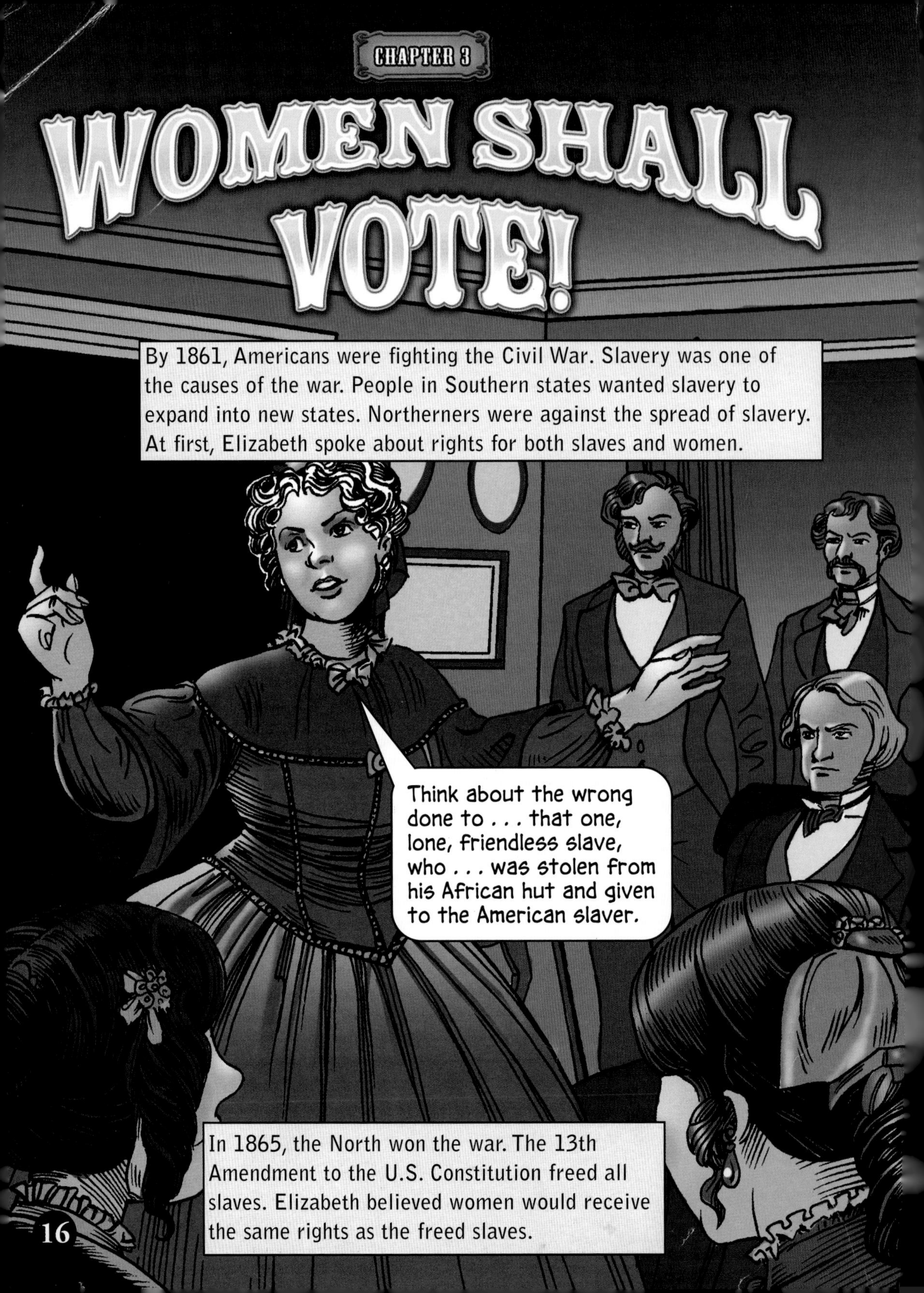
CHAPTER 3
WOMEN SHALL VOTE!
By 1861, Americans were fighting the Civil War. Slavery was one of the causes of the war. People in Southern states wanted slavery to expand into new states. Northerners were against the spread of slavery. At first, Elizabeth spoke about rights for both slaves and women.
Think about the wrong done to . . . that one, lone, friendless slave, who . . . was stolen from his African hut and given to the American slaver.
In 1865, the North won the war. The 13th Amendment to the U.S. Constitution freed all slaves. Elizabeth believed women would receive the same rights as the freed slaves.

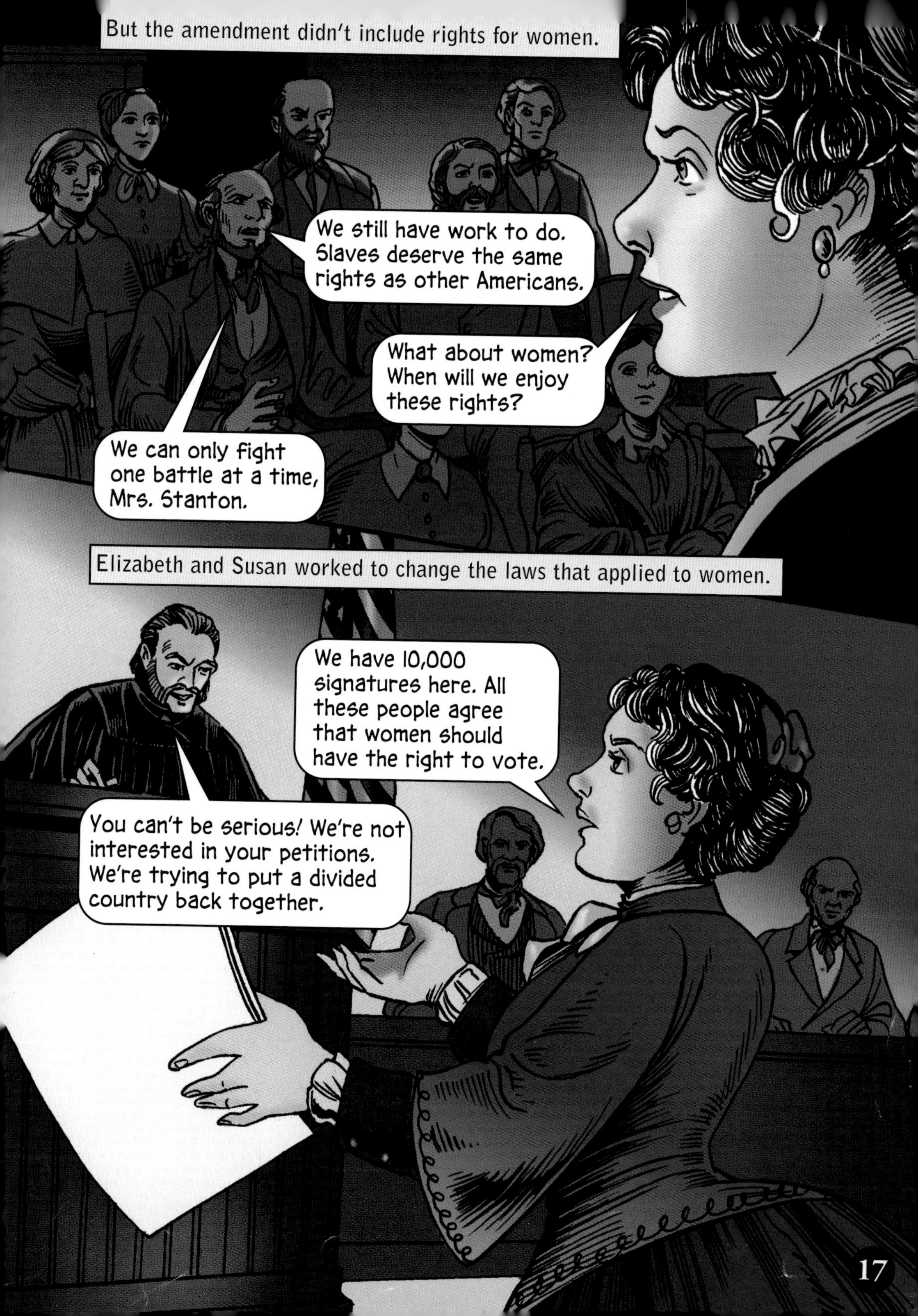
But the amendment didn't include rights for women.
We still have work to do. Slaves deserve the same rights as other Americans.
What about women? When will we enjoy these rights?
We can only fight one battle at a time, Mrs. Stanton.
Elizabeth and Susan worked to change the laws that applied to women.
We have 10,000 signatures here. All these people agree that women should have the right to vote.
You can't be serious! We're not interested in your petitions. We're trying to put a divided country back together.

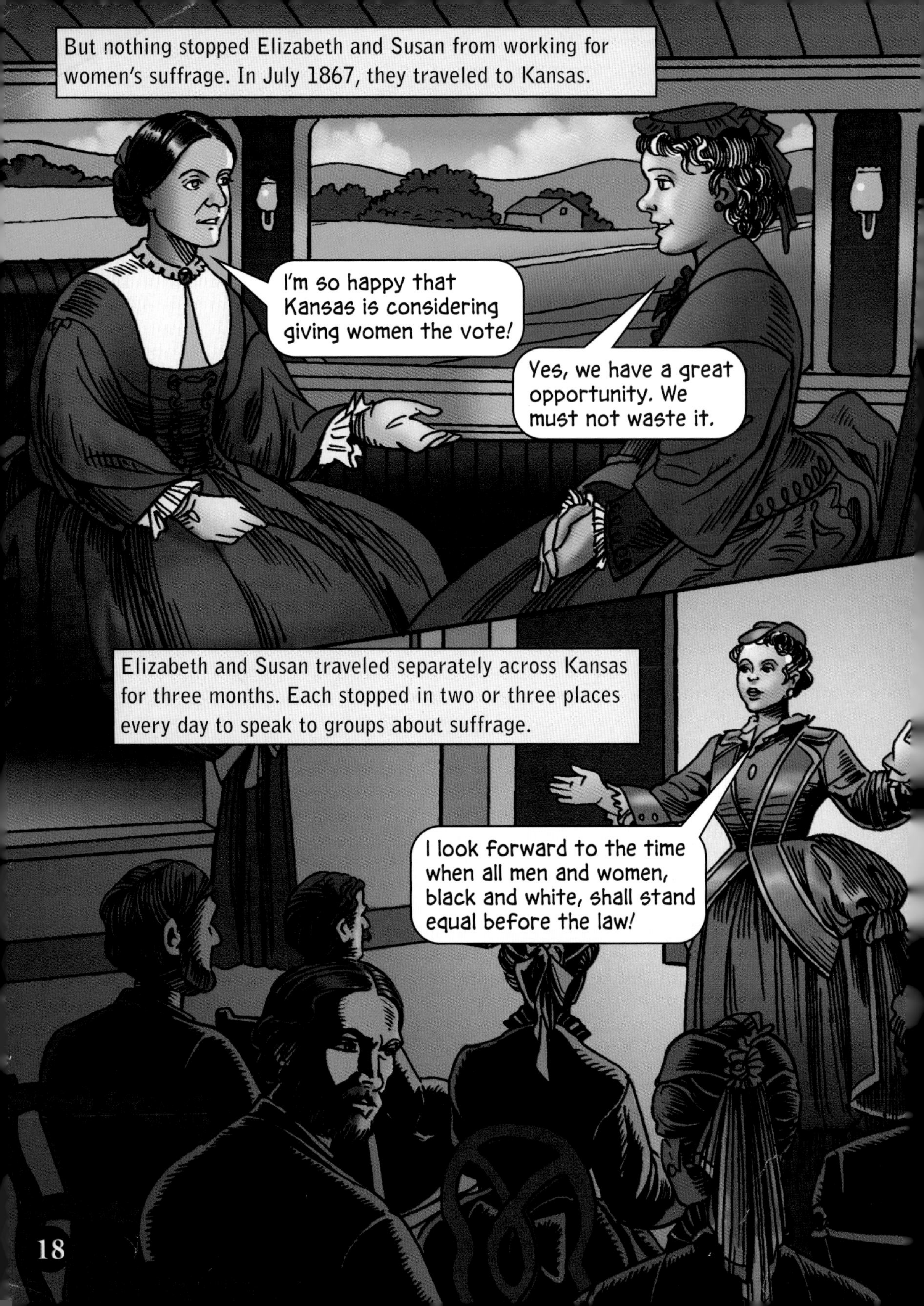
But nothing stopped Elizabeth and Susan from working for women's suffrage. In July 1867, they traveled to Kansas.
I'm so happy that Kansas is considering giving women the vote!
Yes, we have a great opportunity. We must not waste it.
Elizabeth and Susan traveled separately across Kansas for three months. Each stopped in two or three places every day to speak to groups about suffrage.
I look forward to the time when all men and women, black and white, shall stand equal before the law!

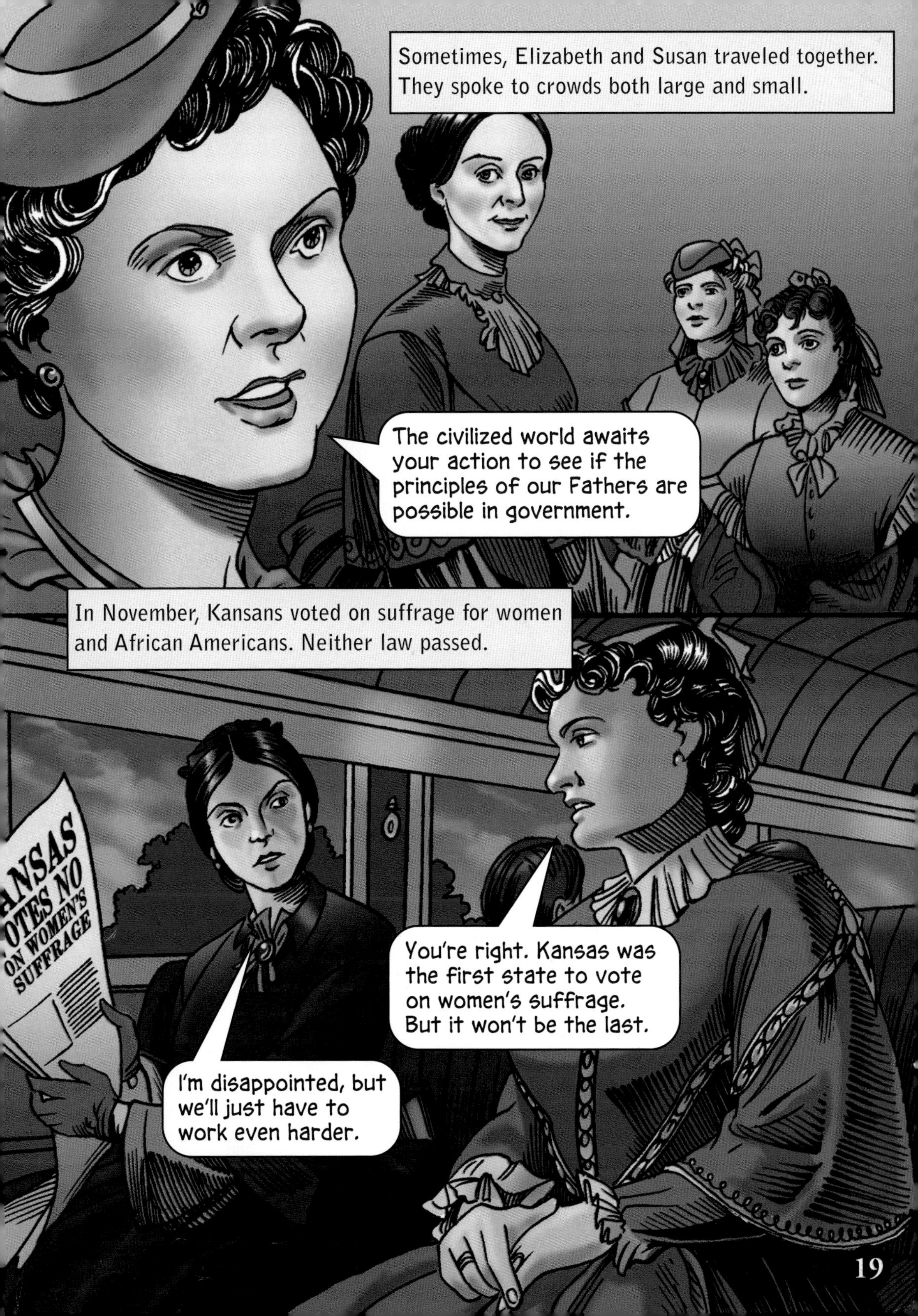
Sometimes, Elizabeth and Susan traveled together. They spoke to crowds both large and small.
The civilized world awaits your action to see if the principles of our Fathers are possible in government.
In November, Kansans voted on suffrage for women and African Americans. Neither law passed.
ANSAS OTES NO ON WOMEN'S SUFFRAGE
You're right. Kansas was the first state to vote on women's suffrage. But it won't be the last.
I'm disappointed, but we'll just have to work even harder.

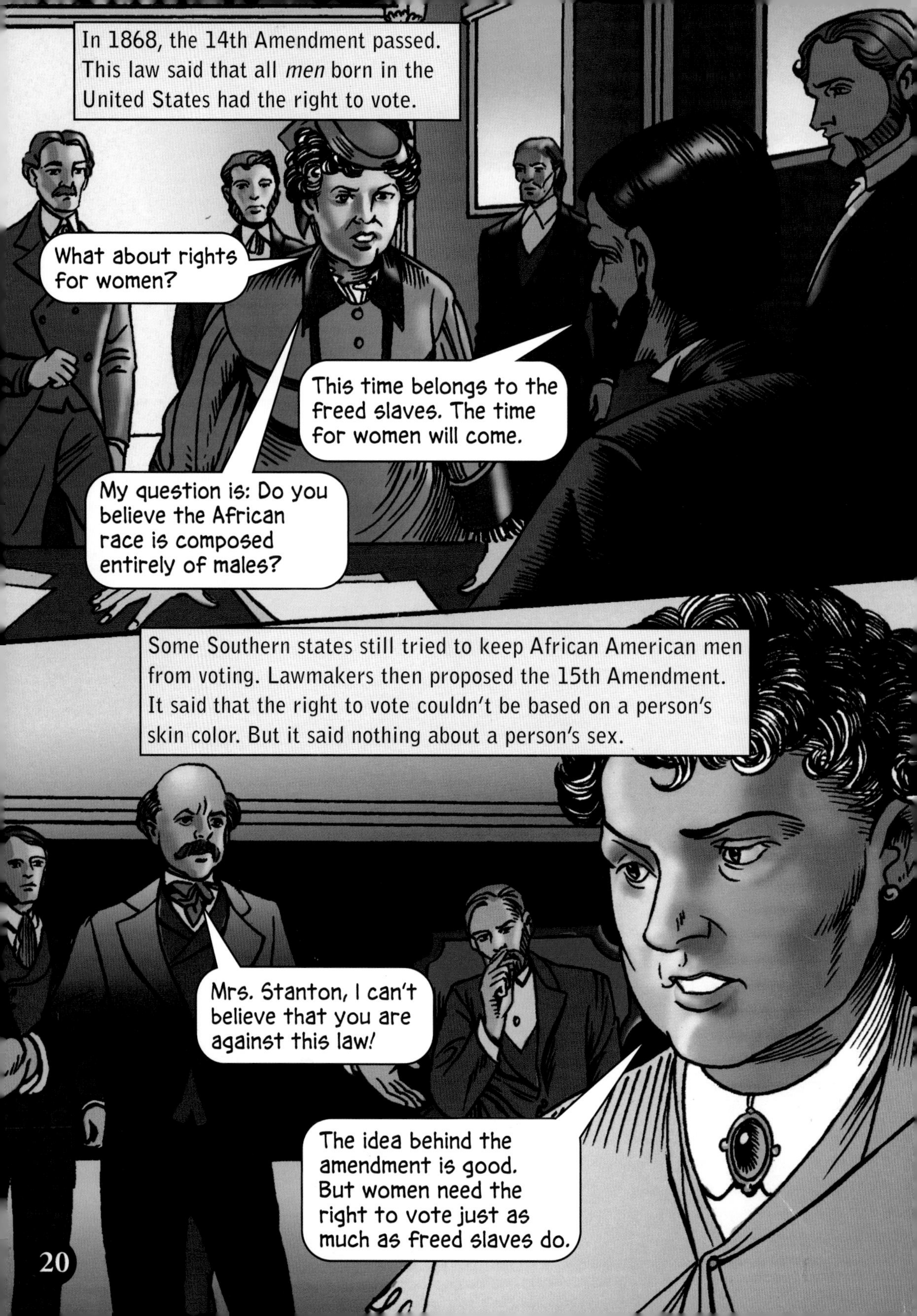
In 1868, the 14th Amendment passed. This law said that all *men* born in the United States had the right to vote.
What about rights for women?
This time belongs to the freed slaves. The time for women will come.
My question is: Do you believe the African race is composed entirely of males?
Some Southern states still tried to keep African American men from voting. Lawmakers then proposed the 15th Amendment. It said that the right to vote couldn't be based on a person's skin color. But it said nothing about a person's sex.
Mrs. Stanton, I can't believe that you are against this law!
The idea behind the amendment is good. But women need the right to vote just as much as freed slaves do.

Many people were angry with Elizabeth for opposing the 15th Amendment. In 1869, the women's suffrage movement split over these differences. Elizabeth led one group. Lucy Stone led the other.

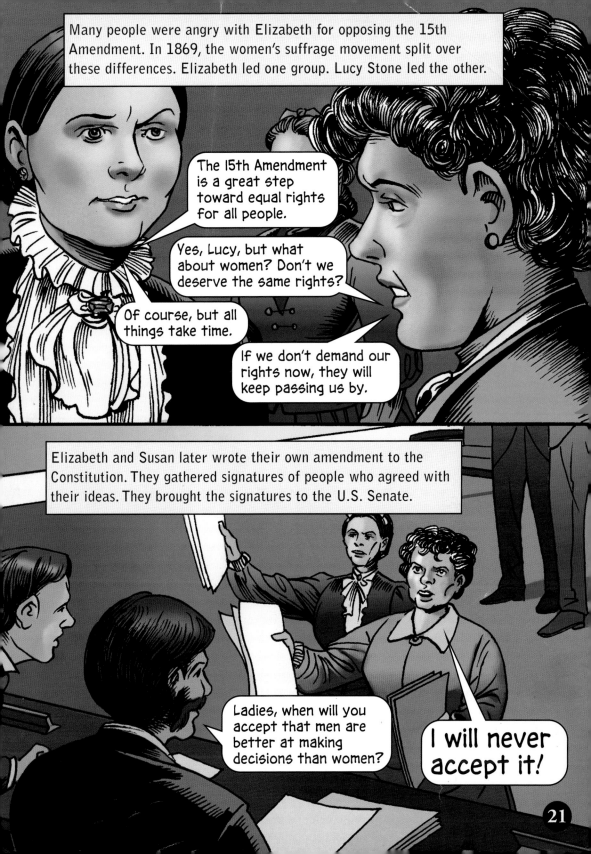

The 15th Amendment is a great step toward equal rights for all people.

Yes, Lucy, but what about women? Don't we deserve the same rights?

Of course, but all things take time.

If we don't demand our rights now, they will keep passing us by.

Elizabeth and Susan later wrote their own amendment to the Constitution. They gathered signatures of people who agreed with their ideas. They brought the signatures to the U.S. Senate.

Ladies, when will you accept that men are better at making decisions than women?

I will never accept it!

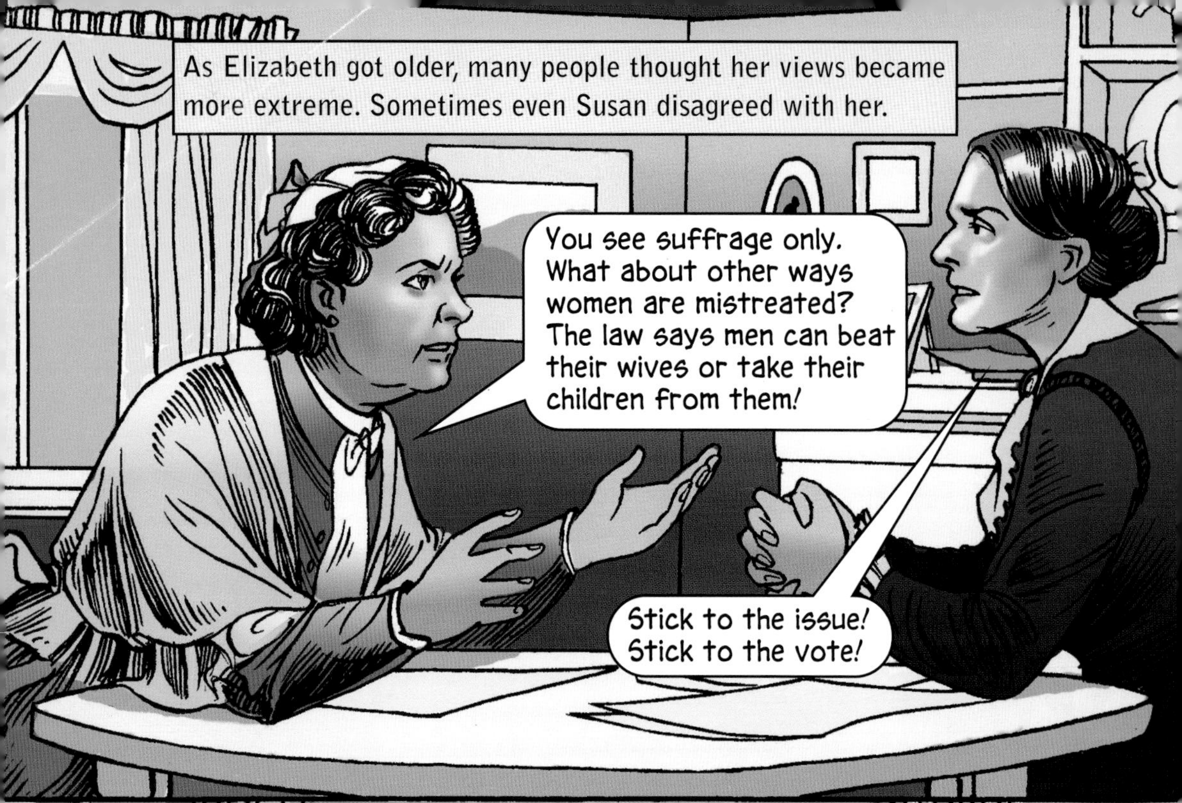
As Elizabeth got older, many people thought her views became more extreme. Sometimes even Susan disagreed with her.
You see suffrage only. What about other ways women are mistreated? The law says men can beat their wives or take their children from them!
Stick to the issue! Stick to the vote!

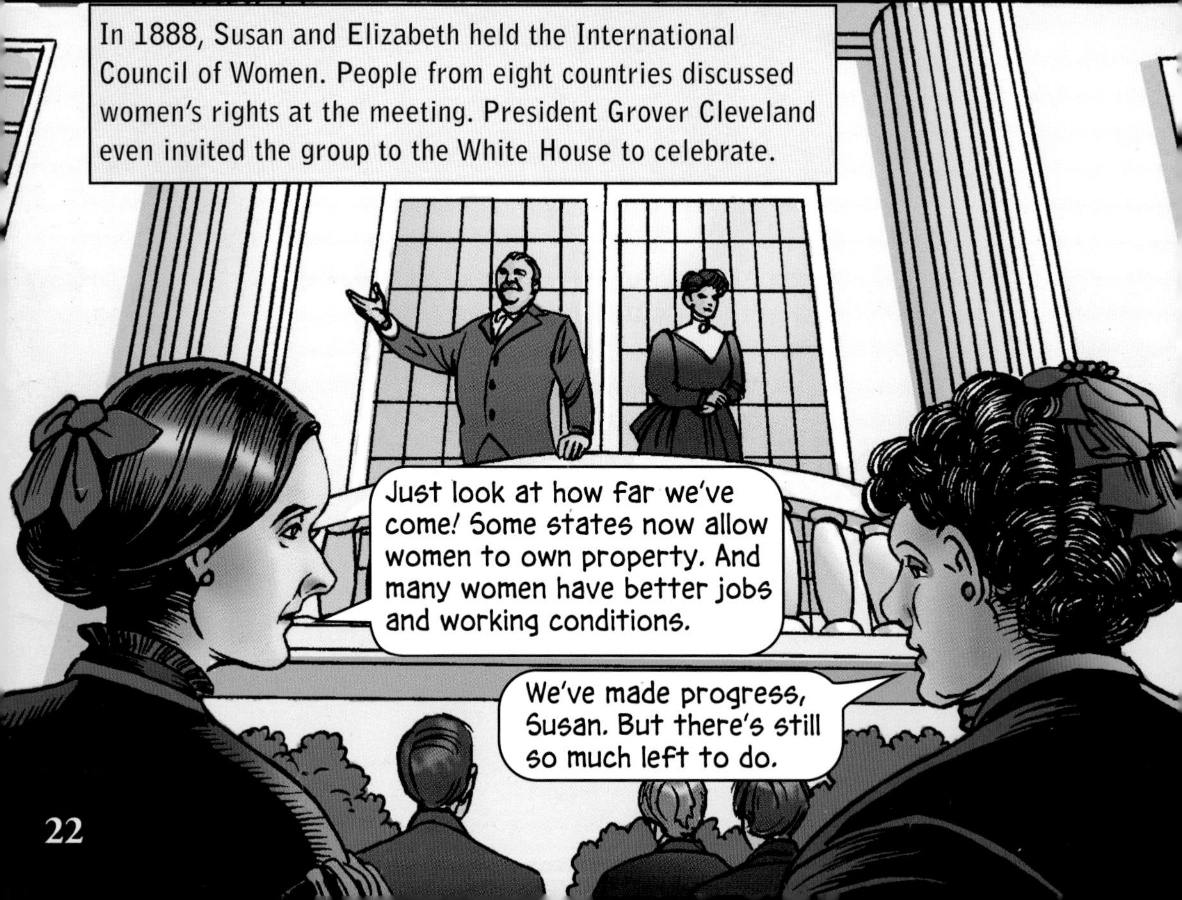
In 1888, Susan and Elizabeth held the International Council of Women. People from eight countries discussed women's rights at the meeting. President Grover Cleveland even invited the group to the White House to celebrate.
Just look at how far we've come! Some states now allow women to own property. And many women have better jobs and working conditions.
We've made progress, Susan. But there's still so much left to do.

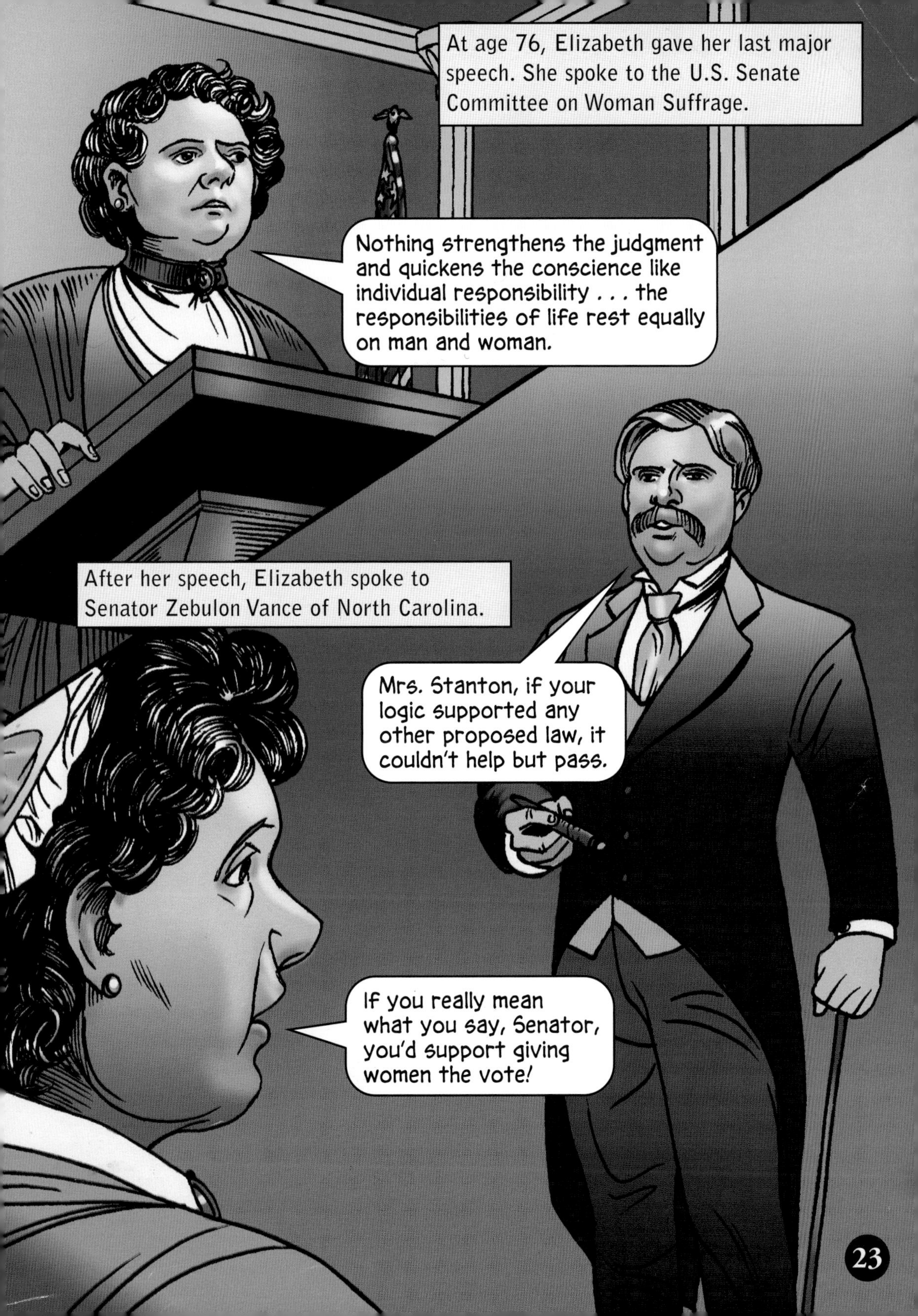
At age 76, Elizabeth gave her last major speech. She spoke to the U.S. Senate Committee on Woman Suffrage.
Nothing strengthens the judgment and quickens the conscience like individual responsibility . . . the responsibilities of life rest equally on man and woman.
After her speech, Elizabeth spoke to Senator Zebulon Vance of North Carolina.
Mrs. Stanton, if your logic supported any other proposed law, it couldn't help but pass.
If you really mean what you say, Senator, you'd support giving women the vote!

CHAPTER 4

ELIZABETH'S LEGACY

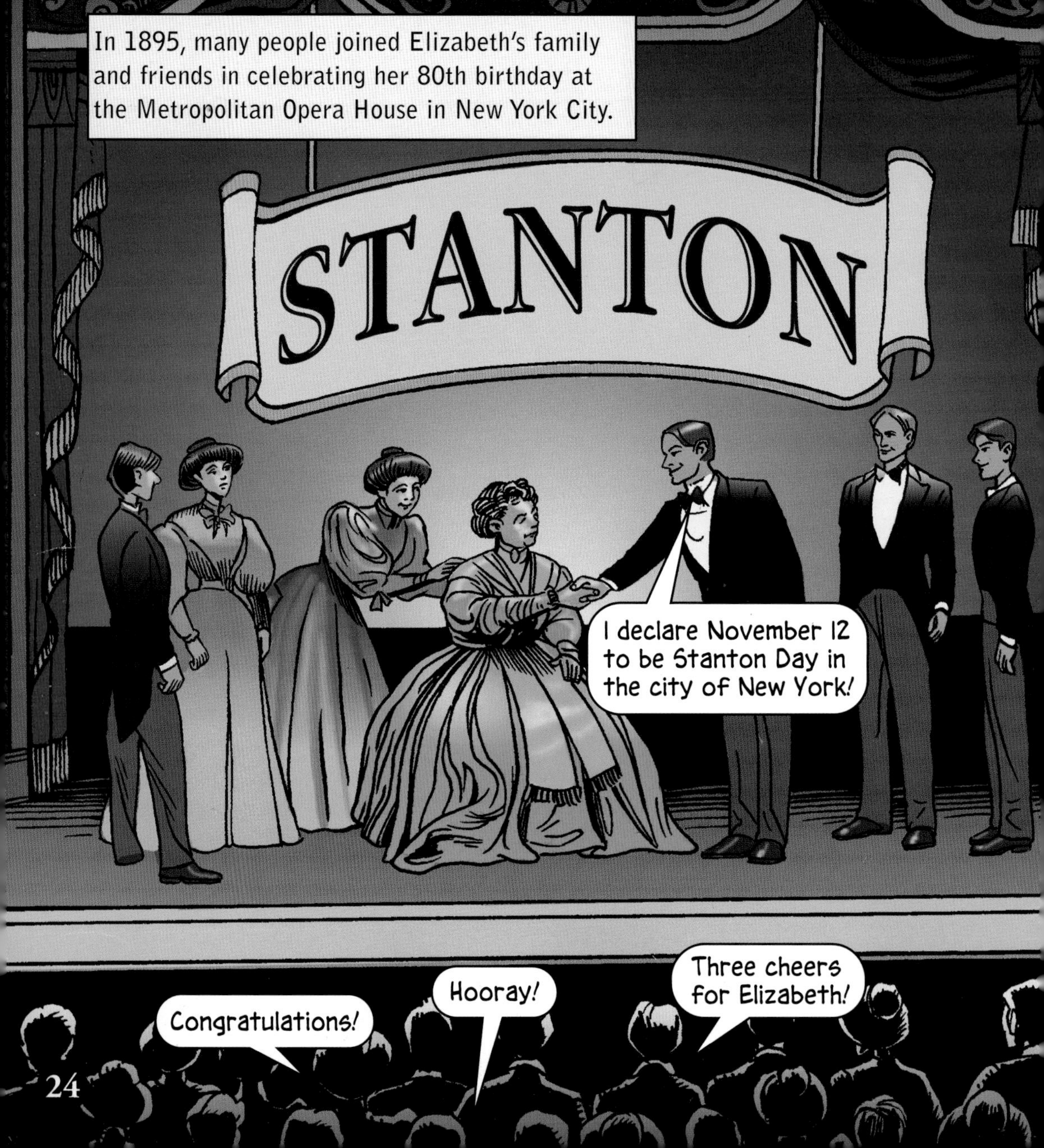
In 1895, many people joined Elizabeth's family and friends in celebrating her 80th birthday at the Metropolitan Opera House in New York City.
STANTON
I declare November 12 to be Stanton Day in the city of New York!
Congratulations!
Hooray!
Three cheers for Elizabeth!

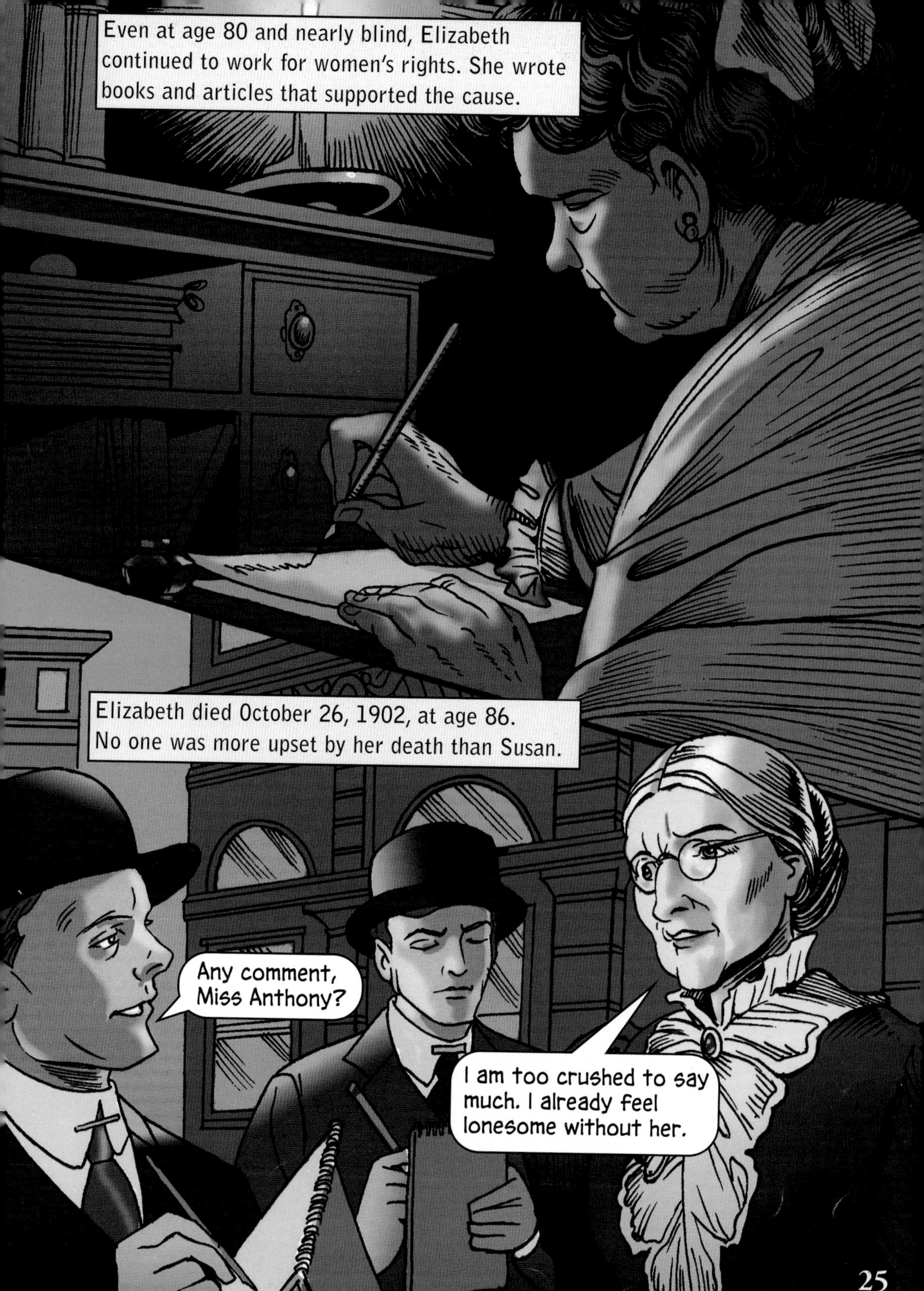
Even at age 80 and nearly blind, Elizabeth continued to work for women's rights. She wrote books and articles that supported the cause.
Elizabeth died October 26, 1902, at age 86. No one was more upset by her death than Susan.
Any comment, Miss Anthony?
I am too crushed to say much. I already feel lonesome without her.

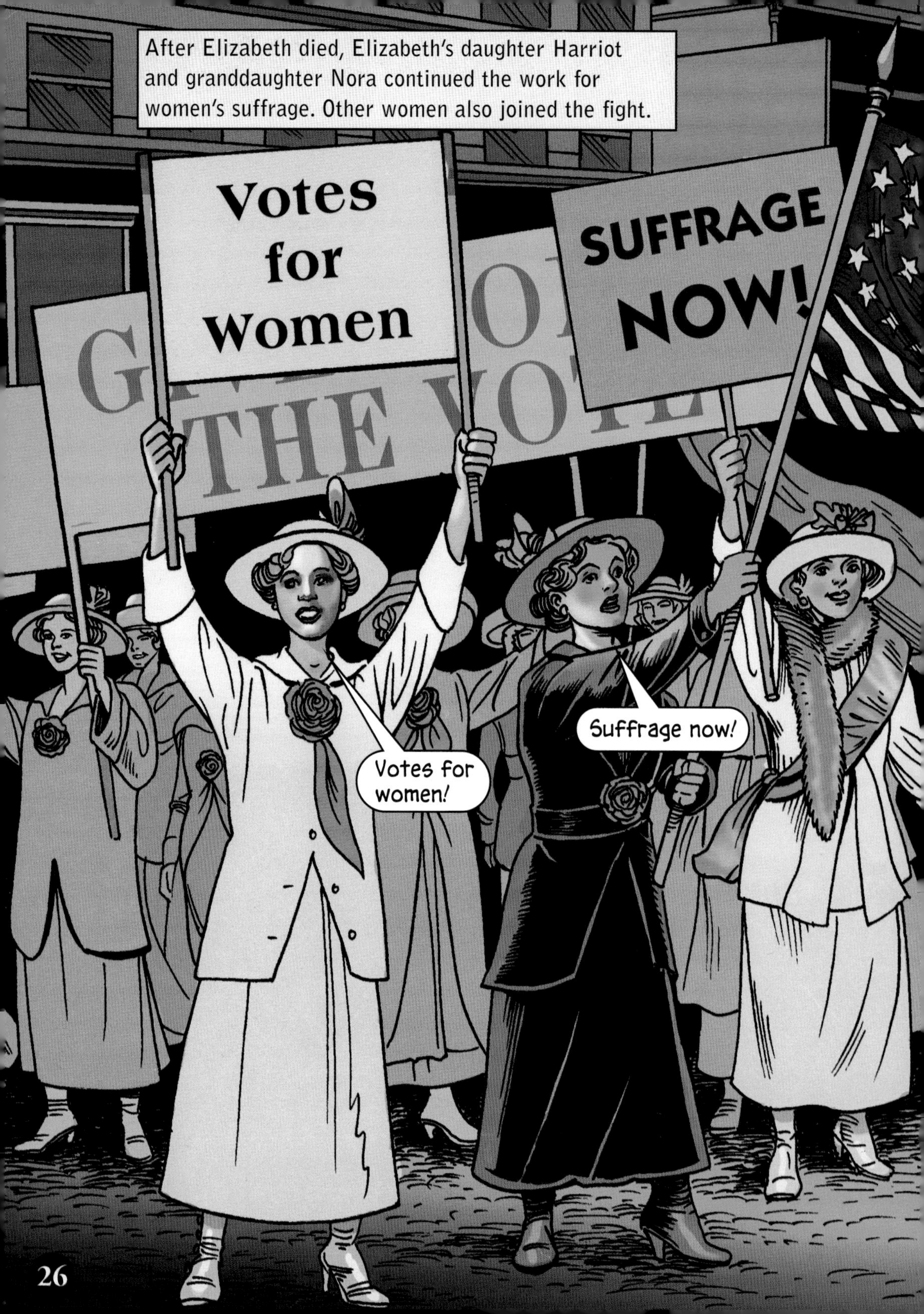
After Elizabeth died, Elizabeth's daughter Harriot and granddaughter Nora continued the work for women's suffrage. Other women also joined the fight.
Votes for Women
SUFFRAGE NOW!
Votes for women!
Suffrage now!

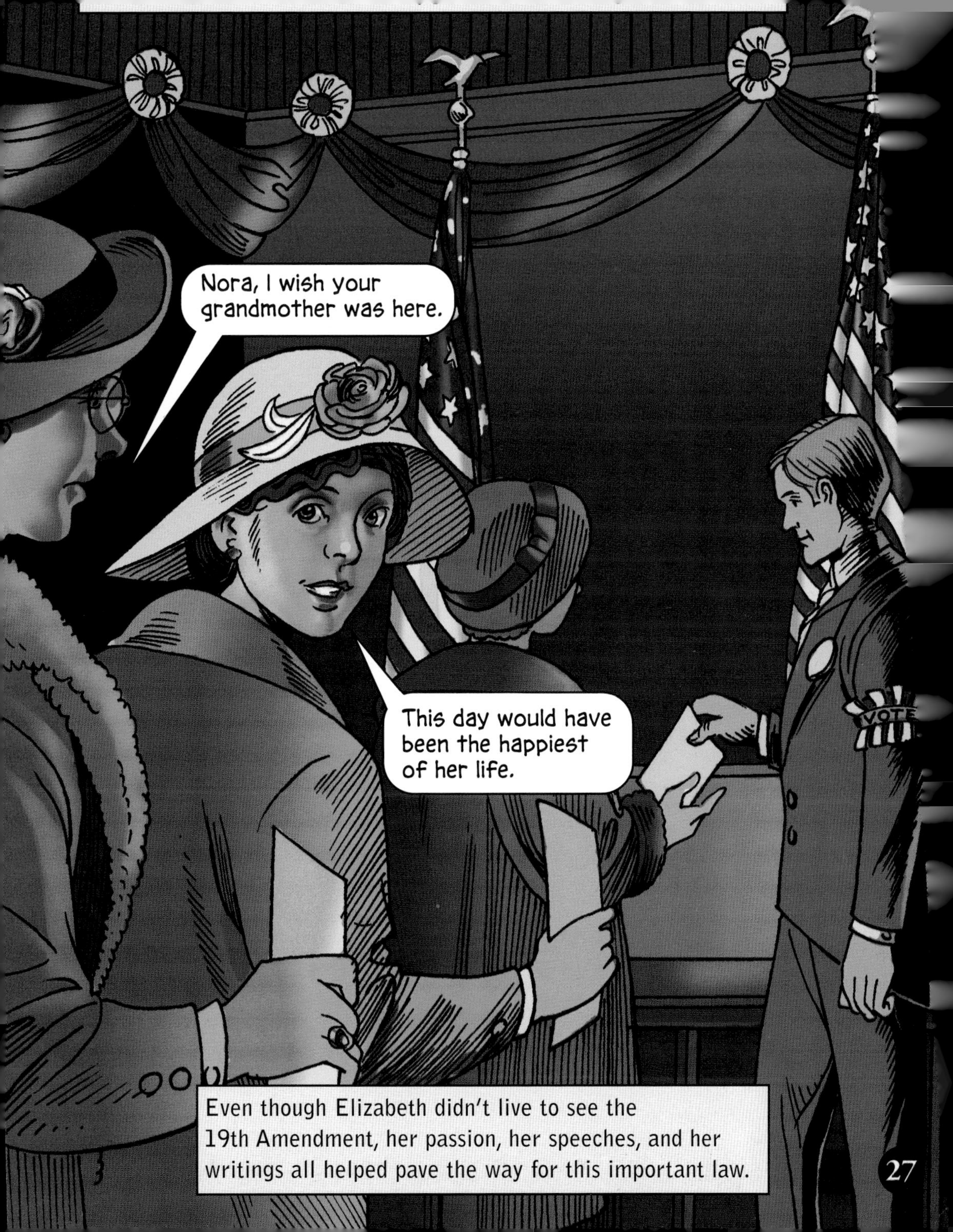
Nora, I wish your grandmother was here.
This day would have been the happiest of her life.
VOTE
Even though Elizabeth didn't live to see the 19th Amendment, her passion, her speeches, and her writings all helped pave the way for this important law.

ELIZABETH CADY STANTON

✓ Elizabeth was born November 12, 1815, in Johnstown, New York. She was one of 11 children.

✓ The Troy Female Seminary in Troy, New York, was one of the first high schools for women. It still exists today. In 1833, Oberlin College opened in Oberlin, Ohio. This college was the first to grant degrees to women and African Americans.

✓ Elizabeth and Henry had seven children. Their sons were Henry, Gerrit, Daniel, Robert, and Theodore. Their daughters were Harriot and Margaret.

✓ Henry Stanton was a lawyer and a newspaper reporter. He also served as a New York state senator. Henry died of pneumonia in 1887.

✓ Famous abolitionist and ex-slave Frederick Douglass attended the Woman's Rights Convention in Seneca Falls. He was one of about 40 men at the convention.

✓ Although Susan had no children of her own, she loved Elizabeth's children. She often helped care for them so Elizabeth could write.

✓ From 1868 to 1870, Elizabeth edited a weekly newspaper called *The Revolution*. This newspaper featured stories about women's rights.

✓ Elizabeth modeled the Declaration of Sentiments on the Declaration of Independence by Thomas Jefferson.

✓ Elizabeth, Susan, and Matilda Joslyn Gage finished writing *The History of Woman Suffrage* in 1880. The book included three large volumes.

✓ In 1890, the two sides of the women's movement joined again. The American Woman Suffrage Association and the National Woman Suffrage Association joined to form the National American Woman Suffrage Association. Elizabeth served as the group's first president.

✓ Elizabeth died October 26, 1902, in New York City.

GLOSSARY

abolitionist (ab-uh-LISH-uh-nist)—a person who worked to end slavery before the Civil War

amendment (uh-MEND-muhnt)—a change made to a law or legal document

convention (kuhn-VEN-shuhn)—a meeting of people with the same interests

petition (puh-TISH-uhn)—a letter signed by many people asking those in power to change their policy or actions

profession (pruh-FESH-uhn)—a job that requires special training

suffrage (SUHF-rij)—the right to vote

INTERNET SITES

FactHound offers a safe, fun way to find Internet sites related to this book. All of the sites on FactHound have been researched by our staff.

Here's how:

1. *Visit www.facthound.com*
2. Type in this special code **0736849718** for age-appropriate sites. Or enter a search word related to this book for a more general search.
3. Click on the **Fetch It** button.

FactHound will fetch the best sites for you!

READ MORE

Mattern, Joanne. *Elizabeth Cady Stanton and Susan B. Anthony: Fighting Together for Women's Rights*. Reading Power. New York: PowerKids Press, 2003.

Moore, Heidi. *Elizabeth Cady Stanton*. American Lives. Chicago: Heinemann, 2004.

Thoennes Keller, Kristin. *The Women Suffrage Movement, 1848–1920*. Let Freedom Ring. Mankato, Minn.: Capstone Press, 2003.

BIBLIOGRAPHY

DuBois, Ellen Carol, editor. *The Elizabeth Cady Stanton–Susan B. Anthony Reader: Correspondence, Writings, Speeches*. Boston: Northeastern University Press, 1981.

Griffith, Elisabeth. *In Her Own Right: The Life of Elizabeth Cady Stanton*. New York: Oxford University Press, 1984.

Stanton, Elizabeth Cady. *Eighty Years and More (1815–1897); Reminiscences of Elizabeth Cady Stanton*. New York: Source Book Press, 1970.

Ward, Geoffrey C. *Not For Ourselves Alone: The Story of Elizabeth Cady Stanton and Susan B. Anthony: An Illustrated History*. New York: Alfred A. Knopf, 1999.

INDEX